Albert Venn Dicey

Letters on Unionist Delusions

Albert Venn Dicey

Letters on Unionist Delusions

ISBN/EAN: 9783744717175

Printed in Europe, USA, Canada, Australia, Japan

Cover: Foto ©ninafisch / pixelio.de

More available books at **www.hansebooks.com**

LETTERS

ON

UNIONIST DELUSIONS

BY

A. V. DICEY, B.C.L.

VINERIAN PROFESSOR OF ENGLISH LAW IN THE
UNIVERSITY OF OXFORD
AUTHOR OF 'ENGLAND'S CASE AGAINST HOME RULE'

(REPUBLISHED FROM 'THE SPECTATOR')

London

MACMILLAN AND CO.

AND NEW YORK

1887

Printed by R. & R. CLARK, *Edinburgh*,
October 1887.

PREFACE

THESE letters are addressed to one class of readers alone, and are written solely with one object.

They are addressed exclusively to Unionists who (forming, as they do, the majority among the electors of the United Kingdom) hold that the creation of a separate Parliament and a separate Executive for Ireland is opposed alike to the duty and to the interest of Great Britain.

The sole aim of these letters is to expose errors or delusions which impede the action and diminish the power of the Unionist party. These errors assume various forms, they all, however, flow from one source; they originate in the failure of Unionists to realise the import and the character of the struggle in which they are engaged. Unionists are carrying on a conflict not for any ordinary party object, but to repel the assaults of revolutionists whose efforts menace the integrity and the power of the United Kingdom. Every question therefore of policy as it arises must be determined by every Unionist with reference to its effect on this conflict. This consideration makes the differences between Liberal Unionists and Conservative Unionists of small moment. This consideration also justifies Unionists in supporting all measures necessary for enforcing the supremacy of the law throughout every part of the United Kingdom. It will also supply the answer to the questions which may be forced by Separatists upon the attention of the nation, namely, whether trial by jury can be retained in a country where the conditions for its fair working are to a great extent absent, and whether Parliamentary representation conferred for the purposes of fair debate may not justly be suspended when it is systematically employed for the purpose of lowering the dignity and destroying the efficiency of Parliament.

These letters are reprinted from the columns of *The Spectator*. They are presented to the reader substantially in the form in which they originally appeared. They share the defects which all but inevitably mark letters written for the periodical press. A kind of composition in which brevity and clearness are matters of necessity hardly admits of the reserves, qualifications, and explanations appropriate to an elaborate treatise. If it be asked why the letters are republished at the present moment in a form of which the author admits the defects, the answer is that they are reprinted for the same reason for which they were originally written; because they may, it is thought, at the present time and in their present shape, be of some service to a cause which the writer, in common with every other Unionist, holds to be the cause of justice and of sound national morality.

A. V. DICEY.

CONTENTS

LETTER I

On Mr. Gladstone's "Concessions" . . . 1

LETTER II

On the Belief in a Compromise . . 12

LETTER III

On the True Danger of Home Rule . 27

LETTER IV

Will Home Rule bring Peace to England? 42

LETTER V

On the Belief in Local Self-Government 59

CONTENTS

LETTER VI
ON THE FEAR OF ALLIANCE WITH CONSERVATIVES 68

LETTER VII
ON THE TWO ALLIANCES 82

LETTER VIII
CONCLUSION 98

LETTER I

ON MR. GLADSTONE'S "CONCESSIONS"

It is time we Liberal Unionists should clear our minds and our language alike from cant. Delusions are prevalent among us which may bring our cause to ruin. Let me to-day note one which is full of pressing danger.

Certain concessions, it is habitually assumed, exist which, if made by Mr. Gladstone, would reunite the Liberal Party. Whether he will make them or has made them is matter of controversy; the oracle is assuredly not dumb, but oracular deliverances admit of diverse interpretations. That, however, the concessions, if made, would reconcile all honest Liberals to Home Rule is, to judge from current talk, past dispute. Yet to any man who stands outside politics and bestows on an important matter half an hour's patient thought, nothing can be clearer than that the so-called "concessions" will not cure, and ought not to cure, the divisions among Liberals.

The concessions obtained or expected from Mr. Gladstone are, to deal only with the most important, twofold.

Mr. Gladstone, we are told, will pledge himself that not one penny from the resources of the United Kingdom shall be spent or risked in compensating Irish landlords for lands or rents taken from them by the action of the State; the policy of the Land-Purchase Bill, grounded as it was on a sentiment of justice or of honour, is to be given up; English taxpayers are to be assured that if they suffer in character they shall not suffer in pocket. This is the noble concession which will conciliate men of common pride and common honesty. It is heralded in with triumph by politicians who boast their descent from the reformers of a past generation. Yet the English Abolitionists rightly preferred that England should pay twenty millions, rather than that the emancipation of the slaves should be tarnished by the suspicion of injustice to slave-owners; our fathers cared for the greatness of England; they knew that Imperial greatness is bound up with Imperial honesty. This modern policy of meanness will miss its aim. The people of England are not niggards. Men fighting for the unity of the nation will not hate Disunion the less because it is coupled with national discredit. Honour is still something, nor is honour alone at stake. Precedent goes for much; wrong done to landowners in Ireland means insecurity to the owners of every kind of property throughout the United Kingdom, and any man who owns a house may be made to understand that his right to be compensated when a Railway

Company takes his shop or his residence, rests on the same basis of morals or of custom as the claim of a landlord to be paid for property taken from him for the benefit of the State. In this matter at least honest Home Rulers and honest Unionists will be found to be at one. The supporters of a policy recommended to them by a semblance of generosity will resent its degradation by connection with the reality of dishonest parsimony.

Mr. Gladstone will, it is asserted, pledge himself that the proposed Parliament at Dublin shall not rob Westminster of Irish representatives.

This is the concession which Liberal Unionists are expected to hail with delight. What is the blessing which it secures us? Neither more nor less than this : that Mr. Parnell and his followers will, after passing laws for Ireland uncontrolled by English interference, take their part in legislating for England. Englishmen will give up governing Ireland, but the Parnellites will still govern England. Nor do the benefits to England of the proposed arrangement end here. Irish members will not, when at Westminster, confine their attention to British or to Imperial affairs. They will keep their eyes fixed upon Ireland; they will be driven not by any natural perversity, but by the force of circumstances, to bend their whole energies to the prevention of English interference in the affairs of Ireland, and to the nullification of all checks placed by a paper Constitution on Irish independence. How this end will be achieved we all know. The Irish representatives will practise their own Parliamentary arts; they will hold the balance between English parties; they will foster English partisanship; they will play as they have played on the mean ambitions of English statesmanship; they will enfeeble the action of the British Parliament; they will take care that oppression or insurrection at Dublin is reinforced by obstruction at

Westminster. If Mr. Parnell had refused Home Rule unless it were accompanied by the retention of the Irish representation in the British Parliament, all England would have been up in arms at Irish unreasonableness. A plan too unfair to have been proposed by the boldness of Mr. Healy, is to be termed a generous concession when forced upon the pliancy of Mr. Gladstone.

The concession, it will be urged, is made in deference to the request of Unionists. This plea may for a moment satisfy disputants in search of a verbal triumph. But in the eyes of any man who looks at facts instead of words, the apology is futile. The case stands thus :—Mr. Gladstone was last year placed in effect in this dilemma: "If you do not," said his opponents, "retain the Irish representatives at Westminster, the sovereignty of the British Parliament will be, under the terms of your Bill, no more than a name; if you do retain them, Great Britain will lose the only material advantage offered her in exchange for the local independence of Ireland." Gladstonians, in substance, replied that the devices embodied in the Government of Ireland Bill at once freed the British Parliament from the presence of the Parnellites, and safeguarded the sovereignty of the British, or (for in this matter there was some confusion) of the Imperial Parliament. On the latter point issue was joined. The other horn of the dilemma fell out of sight, and some Unionists, rightly believing that the Bill as it stood did not preserve the supremacy of the British Parliament, pressed the Ministry hard with all the difficulties involved in the removal of the Irish Members. In the heat of debate speeches were, I doubt not, delivered in which the argument that you could not, as the Bill stood, remove the Irish Members from Westminster and keep the British Parliament supreme in Ireland, was driven so far as to sound like an argument in favour of, at all costs, allowing Members from Ireland to sit in the English Parliament. Those who appeared to fall into this error were, it must be noted, but a fraction of the Unionist Party, and their mistake was little more than verbal. When the Ministry maintained that the removal of the Irish Members from Westminster was a main feature of their Home-Rule policy, opponents naturally insisted upon the defects of the scheme laid before them, and did not insist on the equal or greater defects of a plan which the Government did not advocate. Mr. Gladstone, we are now told, has changed his position, and assents to the principle that Ireland must be represented in the British Parliament. If this assent be represented as a concession to the demands of Unionists, my reply is that it is no such thing. It is merely the acceptance of a different horn of an argumentative dilemma. Grant for the sake of argument (what is by no means certain) that the supremacy of the Imperial Parliament is really saved. The advantage offered to England in exchange for Home Rule is assuredly gone. My friend, Mr. John Morley, used to argue in favour of Home Rule from the necessity of freeing the English Parliament from Parnellite obstruction. As a matter of curiosity, I should like to know what he thinks of a concession which strikes his strongest argumentative weapon out of his hands. My curiosity will be satisfied on the same day which tells us Lord Spencer's reflections on the surrender of the policy represented by the Land-Purchase Bill. Meanwhile, I know well enough the thoughts of every Unionist who is not tied by the exigencies of his political antecedents or utterances. To say that in the eyes of such a man the proposed concession is worthless, is to say far too little. It is not a concession which he rates at a low price; it is a proposal which he heart and soul condemns. What concessions from Home Rulers will, it may be asked, satisfy Liberal

Unionists? The answer is simple,—None. The maintenance of the Union and the repeal of the Union are as inconsistent in fact as they are in logic. The only concession which can or ought to satisfy a Unionist is the surrender of the claim for Home Rule. The simple truth is, that the case is one not for compromise but for conflict. Neither an honest Unionist nor an honest Separatist—and there are honest men enough ranged on each side in this battle—can think of parley. Unionists, at any rate, should recognise that the idea of asking for concessions is no better than a delusion.

The special concessions offered are, to sum the whole matter up, worse than illusory. The Gladstonian policy possessed, with all its radical defects, two merits. The Land-Purchase Bill was an attempt to save English honour; the removal of the Irish Members from Westminster was an attempt to reinvigorate the British Parliament. The policy of Home Rule is made not better, but infinitely worse, by concessions which entail dishonour on the English nation and weakness on the English Parliament.

LETTER II

ON THE BELIEF IN A COMPROMISE

No idea more disastrously weakens the hands of Unionists than the belief that the Home-Rule controversy can be closed by a compromise; that the wishes of Nationalists may be gratified by the creation of an Irish Parliament, whilst the fears of Unionists are assuaged by precautions which deprive the Irish Parliament of all independent and effective authority; that, in short, Unionists, Gladstonians, and Parnellites may all alike accept with satisfaction a new edition of Mr. Gladstone's Government of Ireland Bill, re-edited, amended, expurgated, and, as lawyers say, "settled" by Lord Hartington and Mr. Chamberlain.

The belief is plausible; it is encouraged by the loose talk of leaders who aim at conciliating opposition, it appeals to English love of moderation, it suits our lax habits of thought, it harmonises with the indolence or cowardice of the day. But for all this, the notion that human ingenuity can find a satisfactory halfway house lying somewhere between the maintenance of the Union and the concession to Ireland of genuine Home Rule is a delusion. It is based on two suppositions, neither of which rests on any solid foundation.

The first of these assumptions is that the difference which divides Unionists from Separatists is one which admits of adjustment. To hold this is to shut one's eyes to the nature of the matter in dispute. The maintainers of the Union believe that the United Kingdom is a nation, and has a right to be governed by the voice of its citizens. Home Rulers believe that the claims of Irish nationality are morally superior to the rights of the United Kingdom. The refusal to Ireland of a separate Parliament is the outward and visible sign of the unity of the United Kingdom. The creation of an Irish Parliament endowed with even the most limited powers, would be an open acknowledgment that the Home-Rule controversy had been morally determined in favour of the Irish Nationalists. No doubt the measure which embodied this decision might be filled with provisos, limitations, and guarantees; it might be called a compromise; but in reality it would be no compromise at all, but simply a surrender masked under the form of grudging and ungracious concession.

The reason why Englishmen fail to see the impossibility of a compromise is worth notice. They have for many years been accustomed to a policy of quiet progressive reform; hence, as regards foreign no less than domestic affairs, they find it difficult to recognise the existence of those revolutionary crises which divide men into hostile armies, between whom arrangement, transaction, or accommodation is impossible. It needed the lifetime of a generation to teach England why it was that Austria and Italy could not come to terms as long as a single German soldier remained in Lombardy. Sensible men used to wonder that France should be divided into Imperialists and Irreconcilables. The War of Secession took Englishmen by surprise and filled them with perplexity. Why should the South, it was asked, break up the Union? Why should the North not let the South part in peace? The one thing which in Italy, in France, in America, English good sense failed to perceive, was the existence of an "irrepressible conflict." The blindness which has made us the worst judges of foreign affairs now vitiates our judgment of domestic policy. We cannot recognise revolution, and we confound a violent demand for revolutionary innovation with constitutional agitation for practical reform. The matter, however, is not one on which at this moment I care to insist further. For though it be, for the sake of argument, granted that a Parliament may be conceded to Ireland without surrendering the very principle which makes it worth while to fight for the Union, the belief in the merits of a compromise involves a second supposition less tenable, if possible, than the belief that essential differences of principle admit of accommodation.

This second assumption is that an incomplete, a limited, a restricted, or narrow form of Home Rule is less injurious to England than such a large and ample measure of Parliamentary independence as, for the moment at least, fully meets the demands of Irish Home Rulers. To put the same thing in another shape, it is assumed that if a Parliament be conceded to Ireland, the more restricted the powers given to it, the better for England. This idea is natural, and commends itself to many

Unionists. At first sight, the supposition seems reasonable that whatever is refused to the Parnellites is gained by Unionists, and that if the Act of Union cannot be maintained, the next best thing to its maintenance is to relax as little as possible the bonds which bind together the islands which still make up the United Kingdom. And this notion would be true as well as plausible, if statesmanship were regulated by the principles of trade. But in matters of national policy we must free ourselves from the ideas of the counting-house; we must adopt broad, liberal, and comprehensive views. In the eyes of a Unionist the policy of Home Rule is so full of danger, that it ought to be resisted by every weapon of constitutional warfare. But if ever resistance should become vain, the object of every Unionist, as, indeed, of every man who cares for the welfare of the nation, should be to make sure that the country reaps all the gains which can by any possibility accrue from a rash experiment. The benefits which Home Rule offers, or affects to offer, are fourfold,—the close of agitation through the satisfaction of Irish demands; the strengthening of England through the increased power of the British Parliament, both in Great Britain and throughout the Empire; the fostering of Irish self-reliance; and lastly, should the Home-Rule experiment fail, such an absolute demonstration of its futility as may convince the English democracy that there is no choice between Separation and Union. No one, it need scarcely be said, is less inclined than myself to hope for these or any other blessings from any measure of Home Rule. What I do assert is, that the hope, well or ill founded, of attaining these advantages is the sole inducement which can be offered to England for adopting a scheme of government which the good sense and the conscience of the nation disapprove. Now a moderate or limited form of Home

Rule deprives England of every chance of obtaining the benefits for the sake of which Parliamentary independence will be granted, if at all, to Ireland. If the authority of the Irish Parliament be curtailed within the very narrowest possible limits, if the Irish Executive be placed under the real and substantial control of the English Cabinet, if the richest and most powerful portion of Ireland be placed outside the jurisdiction of the authority which rules at Dublin, ill-timed caution will produce all the worst effects of rashness. Ireland's demands will not have been satisfied; hence Irish agitation will not even for a time come to an end; hence, further, England will not be delivered from the embarrassments and weakness resulting from Irish discontent; and let it be noted that even were the British Parliament freed from the obstruction of the Irish Members, English constituencies would still be influenced by the Irish vote. England cannot at the same time retain the practical control of the Irish administration and be quit of the harassing responsibility for the government of Ireland If the power of the Irish Parliament is small if the jurisdiction of the Irish Executive is limited, the English Parliament must still legislate for Ireland, and the English Cabinet must still govern Ireland. Home Rule limited by restrictions means, in short nothing else than dual control. Dual control in Ireland will, as in Egypt, prove the most unworkable of arrangements. Dual ownership of land is now admitted to be an unworkable system of tenure. An Irish Parliament will not have sat for two years before all the world perceives that dual government is as dangerous a system as dual ownership. In any event, a scheme which Irish Nationalists may, indeed, accept for the moment, because it gives them, at any rate, an Irish Parliament, but which they will accept under protest, is as unfortunate a basis for concord as the imagination can picture. Half-measures are not safe measures. Concessions intended to extinguish discontent must, just because they do not satisfy the demands of the discontented, stimulate and strengthen agitation. We need not look far afield to see the result of bit-by-bit innovation. The tale of experiments in reforming Irish land tenure is full of warning against the danger which may attend hesitating experiments in Constitution-making. The Land Act of 1870 was intended, I presume, to be a final arrangement; the Land Act of 1870 is forgotten. The Land Act of 1881 was assuredly framed as a final settlement; the Land Act of 1881 is now scouted by its authors. The Land Act of 1887 is avowedly a stop-gap. The agitations of seventeen years leave the law as to the ownership of land in Ireland still in effect unsettled; and men of all parties, who agree in nothing else, are now so far of a mind as to be convinced that bit-by-bit reform in the tenure of land is a mistake, and that a change in the law governing the right to the soil of a country is a revolution which, if attempted at all, must be carried through with boldness, with decision, with rapidity. It were pedantry to force further the parallel between the attempt to reform the tenure of land in Ireland by measures which might not alarm English landowners, and the endeavour to inaugurate Home Rule by a compromise which might soothe the fears of English Constitutionalists. Such a measure, again, cannot from the nature of things stimulate Irish self-reliance, and this for two reasons,—the talents, in the first place, which Irish statesmen should direct to curing the diseases under which Ireland suffers, will, if the powers of the Irish Parliament be limited, be turned towards the easier and more congenial occupation of extracting further concessions from England; any failure, in the second place, of a native Government to ensure the prosperity of the country, will be attributed by Irish and by

English opinion also to the restrictions placed on the Parliamentary independence of Ireland. Hence, lastly, and this is a matter of supreme importance, the experiment of Home Rule will from the first be vitiated, and should it fail, will yield no decisive instruction. If Unionists attribute the failure to the inherent defects of a policy which they have never approved, Home Rulers will as certainly believe, and from their own point of view not without good reason, that the breakdown of the system which they have advocated is due to the fact that their plan has never had a full trial, and that the Parliament granted to Ireland has been restrained from exercising the authority claimed for an Irish Parliament by Irish patriots. I am no admirer of Mr. Gladstone; but in this matter Mr. Gladstone seems to me to see further than converts to Gladstonianism, who, anxious to conceal from themselves their own changes of opinion, extort from their leader concessions essentially inconsistent with the spirit of his policy. The last Gladstonian formula I have read—namely, the necessity of granting to Ireland " the powers necessary for Home Rule to a nationality "—has, indeed, the vagueness of other formulas which have proceeded from the same source, but it contains an element of truth. If Home Rule is to be conceded to Ireland, then the majority of Irishmen must assuredly be given the powers necessary to make them rulers at home.

From this point of view, the Bill for the Government of Ireland may be censured not because it went too far, but because it did not go far enough. Its safeguards, its restrictions, its provisos, were worthless; they hampered the action of England without placing any salutary control on the action of Ireland. If the day should dawn, ominous of misfortune to England and Ireland alike, when Ireland receives a Parliament of her own, the best model for statesmanship to follow in framing a Constitution for a country which will, in fact, be a Dependency, is afforded by the Constitution of such colonies as Victoria. The gift to Ireland of Colonial independence would make Home Rule something of a reality, would free the Parliament of Westminster from Irish representatives, and would leave to the Parliament at Westminster the only power worth retaining, — the power of annulling by Act of Parliament a Constitution which an Act of Parliament has created. If any one objects that the grant of Colonial independence to Ireland may bring heavy trouble on England, I am not concerned to contradict him; for Home Rule in all or any of its shapes is, in my judgment, full of peril to Great Britain. If the objector urges that to give real authority to the Irish Parliament involves injustice to large bodies of loyal Irishmen, I admit the force of the objection, and take leave to point out that any argument against the justice or wisdom of entrusting true power to an Irish Legislature is, in fact, an argument against every form of Home Rule.

The case then stands thus:—The demand for Home Rule is one which must either be honestly refused or be honestly granted. A compromise between maintenance of the Union and the concession of Parliamentary independence to Ireland is, of all courses, the worst. The so-called compromise is in principle a surrender, and the surrender, because it pretends to be a compromise, is made on terms which deprive concession at once of its grace and of its possible benefits. Turn the matter which way you will, honest Unionists must dismiss all thoughts of negotiation, and fight on for the maintenance of the Union.

LETTER III

ON THE TRUE DANGER OF HOME RULE

"Separation from England is opposed to the interests of Ireland. Hence Irishmen will never desire Separation or national independence. Home Rule, therefore, threatens no serious danger to England."

This line of argument is, in one form or another, pressed by Home Rulers with telling effect upon Unionists. It is not an appeal to rhetoric, but a fair piece of reasoning. Each part of it deserves examination.

That Separation from England is opposed to the interests of Ireland is an important though a much misunderstood truth.

To Ireland independence means ruin. The country suffers from poverty; the severance of the connection with England entails the loss of all the advantages derived, or to be derived, from British wealth and British credit. Popular contentment will, it may be said, produce riches; but what reason is there to suppose that a nation suffering from distress, and divided by differences of religion and of race into hostile factions, will be a contented people? Statesmanship, it is suggested by Nationalists, will develop the neglected resources of the country; the reply lies ready to hand that such latent sources of wealth, if they exist, cannot be opened without a lavish expenditure of capital, and that an independent Ireland is the last borrower to whom money-lenders will entrust their treasures.[1] As civilisation advances, the expensiveness of civilised

---

[1] Sir Gavan Duffy, indeed, believes that the credit of the Irish Government and Legislature "would probably be, and would certainly deserve to be, as good as that of any State in Europe."—*Contemporary Review*, September 1887, p. 26. This estimate of probability will, I suspect, be shared by few economists.

government increases; a State without natural wealth, without acquired capital, without credit, is not a State which, under the conditions of the modern world, can prosper. Separation, again, will not bestow real independence. From the moment when Ireland assumes the responsibilities of a nation, she stands face to face with a neighbour tenfold more powerful than herself. In an armed contest every chance would be in favour of Great Britain. All the constitutional arrangements which hamper English action and protect Irish weakness would be at an end. No Irish Members would obstruct the energy of the British Parliament; the Irish vote would not turn the course of English policy; it is a lighter task to coerce a feeble enemy by means of embargoes, blockades, bombardments, or invasion, than to govern rebellious citizens by means of spasmodic coercion tempered by inconsistent concession. This topic is odious to me as to every citizen of a still united Kingdom. But the defencelessness of an independent Ireland against England is a consideration of such paramount importance that no honest reasoner dare leave it out of sight. Nor need England, if she wishes to control Irish policy, have recourse to war. A hostile tariff would be Ireland's destruction. "If men do not object to Separation, the butter and the eggs, the cows and the pigs, forbid it." This is the language of an ardent Home Ruler. No candid controversialist can deny its truth. Separation is opposed to Irish interests, for it entails material ruin, and does not ensure real independence.

That Irishmen will never desire independence is nothing better than a plausible prediction.

Nations, like individuals, overlook their true interest. France needs England's goodwill; yet French intrigue overtaxes the patience of our Government. Europe perishes under the weight of gigantic armaments; yet no Continental State disbands a regiment or puts a ship out of service. Economists have exposed for more than a century the fallacies of Protection; but the whole world outside England rejects Free Trade. What reason is there for the fancy that the Irish people will always follow the dictates of expediency? The answer is that the supposition is itself irrational. Young Ireland desired national independence, yet Separation from England was in 1848, as it is in 1887, opposed to the material welfare of Ireland. At this moment the Irish masses ask for Home Rule; yet in the eyes even of Gladstonians the demand has, till recently at least, appeared to rest on a mistaken view of Irish interest. Mr. Parnell's English followers support the demand for Home Rule mainly because it is reasonable to grant Irishmen their wish, not because the wish for Home Rule is in itself reasonable. If the majority of Irishmen desire Parliamentary independence when cool prudence counsels the maintenance of the Union, why should not they desire national independence when cool prudence counsels contentment with a separate Parliament? Absolute faith in the regeneration to be worked by independent national life is at the present day a most natural, as it is also (be it, in justice to the Irish people, remembered) a generous illusion.

If, however, the evils which are inseparable from Separation are no guarantee that the people of Ireland will never demand Separation, the manifest gravity of these evils gives reason for the belief that the Parnellites do not aim at, or at this moment desire, the national independence of Ireland. For the sake of argument, more than this may be granted. It may, argumentatively at any rate, be conceded that the Irish masses will follow the counsels of their leaders, and that for some length of time, after the creation of an Irish Parliament, the policy of the country will not be directed towards Separation. This concession may be made the more readily because the current of events suggests that the leaders of an Irish Parliament will seek an end which, if attained, may give them the advantages without involving the losses of Separation. This end is the transformation of the United Kingdom into a Federal State. The advantages which genuine federalism offers to Ireland are obvious. Ireland, whether politically connected with Great Britain or not, must, it is clear, be dependent on her powerful neighbour. Of Ireland's weakness as a nominally independent nation enough has been said already; her position under such a scheme of Home Rule as has been proposed by Mr. Gladstone would be one of admitted dependence. This dependence arises not from the constraint imposed by those feeblest of all chains, the restrictions of a paper Constitution, but from the nature of things. Any polity under which the United Kingdom of Great Britain is linked with

Ireland gives, in fact, supreme power, if not in theory supreme legal authority, to Great Britain. But if Great Britain itself be divided, say, into three States, the position of things is changed. Then there arises a balance of powers; England becomes nothing more than the most powerful State in a federation, and Ireland may play a leading part under that system of compromise, arrangement, or intrigue, which is the weakness of federalism. The doctrine that the voice of the electors of the United Kingdom ought to be decisive is already decried by Gladstonian Liberalism. Scotland, Ireland, and Wales are taught to claim that in matters of moment deference is due to the majority of the nationalities making up what Englishmen had supposed to be a single nation. State rights are already put morally in competition with the supreme authority of the nation; embody the principle of State rights in a federal constitution, and national unity is gone. Among the

States of the Federated Kingdom, Ireland would perform the part which the Irish representation now plays among the parties which distract the Parliament of the United Kingdom. To agitators careless of English greatness no result could be more satisfactory; the goal of Irish agitation may well become not Separation but Federalism.

The conclusion, then, that Home Rule threatens England with no serious peril is unsound; it rests on the implied assumption that the independence of Ireland is the only grave danger to be feared from Home Rule. The assumption is false; the inference falls with it.

Federalism entails on Great Britain far graver risks than Separation. Every consideration which commends a federal form of government to an Irish Nationalist is an argument against a federal form of government in the eyes of an English patriot. If Ireland as the member of a confederacy reaps the gains without the risk of independence,

England as the member of a confederacy suffers the evils of Separation without securing any of its compensating advantages. Federalism strengthens the Parliament at Dublin; it therefore weakens the Parliament at Westminster. The Central Power is, under a federal system, limited by the acknowledgment of State rights; this means that in Ireland the central government is powerless. Divide Great Britain into different States, and Irish statesmanship will have a noble field for displaying those arts which obtain the balance of power for the State that fosters the jealousies of suspicious neighbours; the creation, in other words, of a confederacy will spread throughout the length and breadth of Great Britain the baneful influence of partisanship and intrigue. Irish nationality may, in virtue of a federal form of government, acquire new strength under the name of State Right; but the revolution which rouses into new life national rivalries, which we had deemed were dead, must destroy both the unity and strength of the British nation. To argue, indeed, elaborately that the transformation of the United Kingdom into a body of States, bound together by a federal tie, involves immense danger, and promises no benefit to Great Britain, is to waste time in proving what to any student of constitutions is self-evident. To conceive that a Parliament at Westminster, checked by the rights and pretensions of three, or it may be four, subordinate Assemblies and subordinate Executives, would wield anything like the authority possessed by the sovereign Parliament of the United Kingdom, is to imagine what is in the strictest sense inconceivable. To deny that the institution of a federal system in Great Britain reverses the policy pursued through generation after generation by all the most eminent of English statesmen, is to close our eyes to the course of history. To dream that such a revolution can be carried through without peril, is to overlook every lesson of experience. To point out the gains which a stupendous innovation promises to Great Britain, is a task that must be left to Home Rulers. They have not yet performed it. It is, we may well believe, incapable of performance. These assertions are made with confidence, because they are assertions which a few years ago would have commanded the assent of every English statesman. Before Federalism has become a party dogma which every Liberal must accept under pain of excommunication, let me ask Liberals to reflect on the attitude that they all occupied in 1880. Then the suggestion that the United Kingdom ought to be turned into a Federal State would have been universally held to savour of madness. The projector who had dared suggest it would have scarcely obtained audience. The tendency of English history, he would have been told, went towards unity; the Act of Union with Scotland was the most successful stroke of Whig statesmanship; that Wales had become amalgamated with England was a piece of rare good fortune; the happiness of Great Britain lay in having attained unity earlier than any Continental State; and throughout the whole civilised world great nations are assuming that political unity which had been the origin of English power. Nor would it then have been denied that the absolute and unrivalled supremacy of the Imperial Parliament throughout every portion of the United Kingdom was the visible sign and result of the political unity of the nation, or that to place the Imperial Parliament in conflict with local legislatures was to shake to the foundation the whole fabric of the Constitution. These opinions were accepted as self-evident by the Liberal party of 1880. The small minority who hinted that the exceptional position of Ireland might justify the creation of an Irish Parliament never breathed a word, nor, I believe, entertained a thought of impairing the unity of Great

Britain. Is there any reason why changes deemed full of danger in 1880 should be thought harmless or beneficial in 1887? I know of none. The exigencies of controversy and the logic of events have forced English Home Rulers into new paths. Their original contention was that the policy of Home Rule, as it affected Ireland alone, might be regulated wholly by the wishes of Irishmen. This position is becoming untenable; the blindest begin to see that Home Rule in Ireland involves constitutional revolution in Great Britain. Our Home Rulers, therefore, since they can no longer deny the necessity, must maintain the expediency of this revolution. From Home Rulers they are turning into Federalists. But faith in Federalism adopted under the stress of controversy by men whose faith is assuredly not grounded on knowledge, will never convince a cool critic that Federalism does not mean for England certain peril and possible ruin.

The examination, then, of the argument which soothes the fears of Unionists leads to this result:—Independence is, in truth, opposed to the interests of Ireland; it is possible, though not certain, that Irishmen may not claim national independence. The very circumstances, however, which check the desire for Separation suggest the policy of dissolving the United Kingdom into a Confederation. But Federalism is more dangerous to England than Irish independence. Home Rule, if it does not threaten Separation, does threaten national disintegration. A sick man fears to lose a limb; he will not be greatly consoled by the assurance that his arm may be retained at the risk of his suffering general paralysis.

LETTER IV

WILL HOME RULE BRING PEACE TO ENGLAND?

Home Rule may be a benefit or may be a curse to Ireland; but Home Rule will, it is argued, give quiet and comfort to England. Let a Parliament meet at Dublin, and Englishmen will be freed for ever from the perennial bother and danger of Irish grievances and Irish agitation; the Parliament at Westminster will devote itself to its own business, and will concern itself as little about murders in Kerry or riots at Belfast as about burglaries at Melbourne or rows at Toronto; sacrifice of authority will, in short, bring freedom from responsibility, and a self-governed Ireland will give England as little trouble as self-governed Victoria.

This is the vision of future ease which seduces electors from the Unionist ranks. But, like other hopes raised by the craving to shirk the performance of duty, this vision is a dream and nothing more.

Among the forms which Home Rule may assume one alone offers even a plausible promise of satisfying England's desire for peace. If Ireland obtains a Constitution like that of Victoria, or, if you prefer it, the Victorian Constitution improved by every amendment which the ingenuity of Sir Gavan Duffy can invent, and if Ireland, like Victoria, be completely exempted from the burden of Imperial taxation, then I admit an optimist may hope that Irishmen living at home may become as contented as Irishmen living in Australia, and that England may be able to leave Irish affairs, like other Colonial business, to the benevolent supervision or the beneficent neglect of the Colonial Office. This hope, however, is doomed to all but certain disappointment.

The reason why this is so may be stated in four words—Ireland is not Victoria.

Any one, however, who would understand the full import of this statement must weigh with care four circumstances wherein Ireland must always differ from one of England's prosperous self-governed Colonies.

Parliamentary independence, in the first place, is not demanded by Ireland in the sense in which it was demanded or welcomed by Victoria. We must not be deceived by words. Home Rule is desired not by the whole, but by a majority of the people of Ireland; by the minority it is deprecated or abhorred. Votes must be weighed as well as counted. The minority who regard Home Rule as another name for local tyranny represent the property, the education, the energy, the orderliness, and the honesty of the country. This is a fact no one dare overlook. It is one thing to satisfy, as in 1782, the demands of a nation, it is another to gratify the importunity of a faction. Ireland, in the second place, is separated from Great Britain not by half the globe, but by a few miles. This is one of those matters which every one knows, and which not one man in a thousand duly considers. Place Ireland in the Pacific Ocean, and Great Britain might with ease govern, or rather not govern, Ireland in the same way in which she governs, or does not govern, Victoria. Place Victoria within twenty miles of the English coast, and not all the provisions of the Victorian Constitution would exempt her from the active control of England. Ireland, again, suffers from centuries of calamity and misgovernment; she is harassed by poverty, by discontent, by social divisions, by natural suspicion of England, by unsatisfied and unsatisfiable desires for national independence. The grant of national independence, in the last place, is a concession which, in the judgment of most Englishmen, whether Home Rulers or Unionists, Great Britain can never make to Ireland. The Colonies are loyal to the Empire, and one cause of their loyalty is that they know they can, if they wish it, claim independence. Ireland is more than half disloyal, and Ireland knows that independence is denied her.

From these four circumstances flow results of the utmost gravity.

England cannot, if she would, cease to intervene in Irish affairs. The social condition and the physical situation of the country forbid it. The colonies are left ungarrisoned; a large army must, in any case, be kept up in Ireland. If rival factions come to a trial of strength, England cannot suffer the neighbouring island to be made the scene of a free fight. Belfast, we will suppose, rises against the Government at Dublin; English forces must, in the last resort, quell the insurrection. It is vain to fancy that the English Government will not have to consider whether the insurgents had or had not moral justification for resistance. Disturbance is put down by the intervention of British arms. The British Government must determine what punishment is to fall upon the rebels. The Irish Ministry, members probably of the League, suggest the pardon of all the criminals or martyrs whose violence or heroism has promoted Ireland's Parliamentary independence. The suggestion, from an Irish point of view, may be politic. Does any one suppose that if the Crown adopts it, the English Cabinet will not be held responsible for the act? English wisdom, calmness, or apathy may possibly tolerate lawlessness in a country still governed by the British Crown, though even English philosophy may be severely tried should some reorganised Invincibles assassinate a Lord-Lieutenant; but foreign Powers will certainly not be so good-natured as to hold that the Cabinet of St. James's is not fully responsible for everything done within the limits of what is now the United Kingdom.

Let a war break out between Germany and France. If Irish ports or ships built in Ireland should be made useful to the French Republic, if the Irish Parliament should express sympathy with the French cause, Prince Bismarck will assuredly not keep silence, and his despatches will be addressed, not to Dublin, but to London.

Disappointment always follows reform. To this principle the politics of Ireland form assuredly no exception. But disappointed hopes mean with Irishmen dissatisfaction with England. Nor will discontent, following immediately on the grant of Home Rule, lack reasonable ground. For Home Rule promises Ireland in appearance far more of independence than it can in reality bestow. English interference must generate discontent, and popular disquiet must in its turn make the intervention of England necessary. Englishmen and Irishmen will alike feel disappointment. The dreary story of the years which followed 1782 will in another form, it is likely enough, repeat itself. Englishmen will complain that no generosity satisfies Irish demands. Irishmen will feel that the gifts of England are worthless. As in 1782, both parties will be in the right. Irish independence of England will prove unsatisfactory because it must be unreal; the unreality will arise neither from the perversity of the weaker, nor from the treachery of the more powerful country, but from the fact which all of us are slow to acknowledge,—that the true independence of Ireland, as long, at any rate, as she is part of the British Empire, is an impossibility. Whoever attempts to establish it, fights against stronger forces than those which baffled Grattan. He fights against the centralising tendencies of the age; he is thwarted by the progress of science; he is resisted by the railway, by the steamship, by the telegraph. The nature of things draws Ireland nearer to England. Politicians who would resist the nature of things oppose the providence of God. That the experience of 1782 may repeat itself, is a likelihood; that the tragedy of 1798 may also be re-enacted, is a fearful possibility; Irish resistance to Great Britain will not be the less dangerous because it may be guided by the Irish Parliament and protected by the Irish Courts.

If Home Rule as Colonial independence holds out to England a seductive hope of rest and quiet, Home Rule as Federalism does not even promise repose from agitation, and the movement in favour of Home Rule is turning rapidly into a movement in favour of Federalism.

On Mr. Gladstone's scheme for the government of Ireland as amended, or spoilt, by the concessions to Sir G. Trevelyan, I will make but two observations. To keep the Irish Members at Westminster is to surrender once and for all the hope that Parliament may throw the burden of Irish business off its shoulders. To keep the Irish

Members at Westminster is again to vitiate the whole system of English party government. Is it credible that, when Ireland has, in fact, ceased to be ruled as part of the United Kingdom, English Liberals will consent to England being governed on Conservative principles because Irish Catholics have coalesced with English Tories, or that English Conservatives, when supported by the electorate of Great Britain, will acquiesce in democratic reforms made possible only by English Liberalism allying itself with Irish discontent?

No need, however, to criticise the semi-Federalism of Gladstonian Home Rule. It is but the halfway house towards the conversion of the United Kingdom into a Confederacy; it is the first stage towards the Federalisation of the British Empire. "If the British Empire is to be held together, there must be a Federal Union in which taxation and representation will go together."[1]

[1] *Contemporary Review*, September 1887, p. 30.

These are the words of Sir Gavan Duffy. He is a statesman of experience. He utters this opinion as part of an argument meant to win over English sentiment towards Home Rule. The words are of high importance. They decisively mark the goal towards which the policy of Irish Home Rulers must tend. How many, I wonder, of my readers realise all that the scheme sketched out by Sir Gavan Duffy involves? People speak as if the federalisation of the British Empire were a holiday task. It is in reality the hardest undertaking ever set to himself by a statesman or dreamt of by a doctrinaire. Think for one moment on all that the plan involves. A Constitution must be invented which will suit England, Ireland, Canada, Jamaica, the Cape, Victoria, Mauritius, and a host of other countries divided from one another by distance, no less than by differences of race, of history, of institutions. The Constitution must be one which they are, each and all, willing to adopt. It must have at its head an Executive which they are all willing to obey, and the Executive must be armed with a force which, in case of necessity, can compel the obedience of States as ancient and powerful as England, or as youthful, vigorous, and impatient of control as Victoria. If this Executive is to be the English Crown, then the English Monarch must be made independent of the Parliament of England; if the Executive is to be some new created person or body, then the English Monarch must, for the first time, occupy an avowedly subordinate position in the British Empire. A Federal government will require a Federal army. A Federal government almost necessarily involves the creation of a Federal court. It certainly involves the creation of a Federal Congress which must have power to control in some respects the decisions of every subordinate assembly, whether such an assembly be the Parliament of England, the Parliament of the Canadian

Dominion, or the Parliament of Victoria. A Federal government all but involves a Federal Customs Union, it involves therefore a thorough change in the financial policy both of Great Britain and of her colonies. It will further be necessary to determine the relation of the Confederacy and its Executive to the Indian Empire. This is a question which itself alone is sufficient to task all the political talent which the British Empire can supply. Suppose, however, that a theoretical answer to this and a score more of equally difficult problems be found. Suppose that a satisfactory constitution be framed on paper, the difficulties of British Federalists will be but at their beginning. The English Crown, the English House of Lords, above all, the English House of Commons, must be induced or compelled to make a tremendous sacrifice of authority. The ancient Parliament of England must consent to sink into the legislative assembly of one among a score of States. Under a

Federal Constitution, Great Britain must be forced to surrender supreme authority. Her colonies must be forced to surrender much of local independence. What is the power by which this gigantic revolution is to be accomplished? No one knows. Who are the men who are to carry it through? We all of us know too well. They are none other than our existing English politicians. These are the men who have never dared to attempt the reform of the House of Lords, who find it beyond their capacity to provide London with a municipal Constitution, who hesitate at the creation of County Boards, who cannot maintain the decency of Parliamentary debate, who are paralysed by the obstructiveness of eighty-six Parnellites, who quake before the audacity of Dr. Tanner. Are these the statesmen to whom may be entrusted a task which might well have daunted the boldness of Cavour or Bismarck, and might have overtaxed the statesmanlike inventiveness of the founders of the

United States? The task itself seems to many judges impossible of performance. How this may be I have no call to pronounce.¹ What I do contend is that the mere attempt to carry out the policy of Federalism necessitates an amount of labour and effort which must for years divert the energy and talent of British statesmanship from every other task. Let the English people once sanction the attempt to federalise the Empire, and they may set aside the hope that any attention will be paid by overtasked politicians to such minor matters as the reform of Local Government, the

---

[1] To point out the difficulties of, so to speak, federalising the British Empire is, it should be noted, a totally different thing from arguing or suggesting that nothing can be done to draw closer the connection between England and her colonies. One of the strongest objections to extensive schemes of so-called Imperial Federalism, is that these projects may actually stand in the way of humbler but much more practicable and much more important plans, for a kind of alliance between England and her colonies, which might greatly increase the naval or even the military force of the whole Empire.

regulation of traffic in drink, the housing of the poor, or the providing meritorious rustics with the proverbial "three acres and a cow," or with any of the blessings hinted at by this convenient formula. Any attempt to change from top to bottom the institutions of an ancient and powerful state, will bring upon the English people years of contest, of agitation, of turmoil. English artisans and labourers are promised that if Ireland is allowed to govern herself, the English Parliament will devote its undivided attention to removing social inequalities and to relieving the suffering of the poor. The prospect is tempting, because the people of Great Britain at the present moment care little for political changes, and are deeply interested in schemes for ameliorating the material condition of the population. But the people of England are also told, and not without truth, that Home Rule points to Federalism. If Parliament be engaged in the foundation of a Federal State, even if the effort be confined for the time only to the federalisation of the United Kingdom, Parliament, we may be assured, will have neither time nor power for elaborating schemes of social reform. The advocate of Home Rule asks the English people to enter on wide and unprecedented schemes of constitutional innovation. His suggestions, whether he knows it or not, amount to this, that Englishmen should forego social and economical reforms, on which they set great store, for the sake of trying constitutional experiments for which they care nothing. The proposal is not one which in my judgment will commend itself to English good sense. However this may be, Home Rule as Federalism means not the close of a conflict, but the opening of a Revolution.

Home Rule, then, whatever be its form, offers to England not peace and rest, but disquiet and discord.

LETTER V

ON THE BELIEF IN LOCAL SELF-GOVERNMENT

UNIONISTS of repute believe or hope that the demand for Home Rule may at this moment be met by giving to Ireland a system of extended Local Self-Government. This opinion is one which any Englishman, tormented by the perplexities and annoyances of a bitter political controversy, would adopt with pleasure. It is, however, open to three cogent, not to say fatal, objections.

These objections shall be stated by me with all the brevity I can command; my views on the subject in hand have been already laid before the public in another form.[1] Let me, however, request of candid

---

[1] See *England's Case against Home Rule*, chap. ii., Meaning of Home Rule.

readers that summariness be not mistaken for dogmatism.

First, Home Rulers demand not Local Self-Government, but Home Rule. No one ever satisfied a claim by giving the petitioner something which was not the asked-for boon or right. Local Self-Government and Home Rule, though the ideas easily admit of verbal confusion, are two radically different things. Local Self-Government, as applied to Ireland, means the delegation by the Parliament of the United Kingdom to Irish local bodies, such as town councils, county boards, vestries, and the like, of strictly subordinate powers of legislation for definite localities. Home Rule means the creation of an Irish Parliament with authority to govern Ireland, and to govern Ireland freed from the direct control of the Parliament at Westminster. A Home Ruler desires the political recognition of Irish nationality; it is vain to fancy that he will be satisfied with improvements in parochial or municipal administration. There is, indeed, no necessary connection whatever, though the English public find this hard to understand, between State Rights and Local Self-Government. An Irishman might with perfect consistency hold that Home Rule is the cure for Irish misery, and yet maintain that to increase the power of local bodies would work irreparable evil to Ireland. It is quite possible that an Irish Parliament would vastly increase the powers of the Irish Executive. The French democracy has invariably approved of centralisation, and it were rash for an Englishman to pronounce that Frenchmen are wrong in thinking a strong administration beneficial to France.

Secondly, It is open to the gravest doubts whether the extension of Local Self-Government would benefit the Irish people. If Irishmen, indeed, wished for an increase in the authority of local bodies as for a thing desirable in itself, the existence of the wish would, *primâ facie*, afford a strong argument in favour of its gratification. No proof, however, has been given that Irishmen hold that the country would be better governed if every Irish town council, or vestry, had twice the powers it at present possesses, or if elective county boards administered all the affairs of each county. The Parnellites would no doubt welcome increased municipal franchises; for any increase in the power of local bodies would diminish the power of the English Government. But there is nothing whatever to show that sagacious Home Rulers, and still less that Irishmen who are not Home Rulers, deem that an extension of the authority possessed by local bodies would in itself be a blessing to Ireland; there is fair ground for the supposition that it might be a curse. Local Self-Government requires for its beneficial action the existence of at least two conditions. The inhabitants of the township, or other locality called upon to exercise self-government, must, in the first place, have acquired habits of independence, of honesty, and of taking active trouble in the management of their own affairs; the different classes, in the second place, of the self-governing community must be on terms of neighbourly confidence. Whether these conditions exist in Ireland, I leave to the judgment of my readers. Where these conditions do not exist, local government is but another name for parochial incompetence, parochial tyranny, and parochial corruption. The rule of high-toned officials is possibly inferior to the self-government of a community which chooses for its administrators the ablest and most honest of its inhabitants. But the administration of competent officials is far better than Local Self-Government carried on by local busy-bodies and local intriguers. Put aside all questions of national susceptibility, and any Englishman or Irishman who cared for good administration would prefer the rule of such men as Mr. Burke, Sir Robert Hamilton, or Sir Redvers Buller, to the supremacy of the local politicians who command the confidence of the National League. France, after being tormented by the imbecility and the cruelty of Jacobin Clubs, hailed with delight the competence and comparative equity of the Napoleonic administration. The possibility that under a system of Home Rule Ireland might turn away from revolutionists, and make the best Irishmen the rulers of the country—might, to put the matter in a concrete form, dismiss Dr. Tanner to obscurity, and put Sir Gavan Duffy in power—is, I frankly admit, one of the strongest among Home-Rule arguments. But it is also the strongest of arguments against a policy which, though called extension of self-government, might turn out nothing else than the strengthening of local tyranny.

Thirdly, At the present moment, to extend the power of local bodies throughout

Ireland is to provide agitators with arms for the destruction of the United Kingdom.

Ireland is passing through a revolutionary crisis; her whole social system is shaken; the tenure of land is in course of modification; the people are suffering from misery, and have been for years excited by political agitation. To increase the power of corporations, boards, or vestries, is at this juncture to cause a twofold evil. The first evil is, that municipal franchises must of necessity be exercised wholly with a view to political objects; men must be elected mayors, councillors, or guardians, not because of their administrative capacity, but because of their zealous or fanatical partisanship. The second evil is, that powers conferred for the government of cities or of counties can be used, and from the nature of things will be used, to impede the action of the Executive. The Jacobins became despots because French reformers, by conferring excessive authority on separate municipalities, enabled conspirators to oppose the moderating control of the Central Government; whilst Jacobins were in opposition, Jacobins favoured that kind of Local Self-Government which enfeebled the Executive. In this matter, however, we need not seek historical or foreign examples. Recent experience, or the observation of events passing before our eyes, may show us how naturally revolutionists use the rights of Corporations or of Boards of Guardians to weaken the power of the National Government. Whoever argues in favour of increasing the sphere of Local Self-Government in Ireland should state how the Lord-Lieutenant could maintain order in Dublin if his power were balanced by the immensely increased authority of the Lord Mayor.

The name of "Self-Government" has a natural fascination for Englishmen; but a policy which cannot satisfy the wishes of Home Rulers, which may—it is likely enough—be of no benefit to the Irish people, which will certainly weaken the Government in its contest with lawlessness and oppression, is not a policy which obviously commends itself to English good sense.

LETTER VI

ON THE FEAR OF ALLIANCE WITH CONSERVATIVES

"No Liberal ought to support a Conservative Government." This maxim is rarely stated in its naked absurdity by any man with pretensions to intelligence unless he be a candidate fighting for a seat. But for all that, it is a doctrine which turns elections, and clouds the judgment or disturbs the conscience of many a Unionist. It is worth while, then, to point out the several objections which are fatal to this precept of party loyalty.

It rests on a false estimate of the condition of the public opinion and of the relation between the political parties of modern England.

It assumes that there exists a coherent body of admitted Liberal truth opposed to a rival body of Conservative error; that Liberal orthodoxy or Conservative heterodoxy is the faith of every Englishman; that the members of opposed parties look upon their opponents with deep hostility, and that in the world of politics, as in the world of theological controversy, transition from one camp to another savours of treachery, or excites, at any rate, that disapprobation which popular judgment or prejudice attaches to conversion from one form to another of religious belief. There have been times when this condition of opinion existed. In 1829 Dr. Arnold, if I remember right, thought that political animosity might engender civil contests. But we are living in 1887, not in 1829, and the terms which might describe the divisions of fifty or sixty years back do not even fairly caricature the present state of public sentiment. Neither Liberals nor Conservatives can boast a definite and distinct creed. Who dares define the orthodox Liberal doctrine as to female suffrage, as to proportional representation, as to the proper relation between the authority of the State and the rights of individuals? On each of these points, and on half a dozen more "fundamentals," Liberal opinion is divided. On each of them we may find some Conservatives who agree with some Liberals and disagree with other Conservatives. This absence of definite formulas should excite neither wonder nor censure. Liberalism and Conservatism have for half a century been discriminated from each other by the distinction between democratic and anti-democratic principles. Democracy has triumphed; her victory has effaced old lines of demarcation. This is no mere external change; let it be charged to no one on any side as dishonesty. All of us have yielded to the complex influences which men call the spirit of the age. Differences lying deep in human nature will no doubt again make their appearance on the field of political life. "Gratuitous prediction is gratuitous rashness; otherwise, an observer might risk the prophecy that a time of bitter conflict is at hand. All I assert is that the vital oppositions of sentiment which sever citizens into hostile armies do not coincide with the boundaries which part modern Liberalism from modern Conservatism. Nor can the distinction between Liberals and Conservatives be identified with the distinction between the party which does possess and the party which does not possess a good character. In England it has often occurred that the repute of a particular political connection for sobriety, prudence, integrity, and conduct, has sunk so low that the party has missed power neither from lack of talent nor from the essential unpopularity of its principles, but from want of credit. Fifty years of weakness was the penalty paid by the Whigs for having lost, under the guidance of Fox, the attributes summed up in the term "respectability." Distrust of Disraeli robbed the Conservatives for a generation of the influence which should naturally have accrued to them during a period of quiescence destined to find its representative in Palmerston. In England, the party of morality and of conduct has always in the long run become the possessor of popularity and of power. This is a truth to be commended to the serious meditation of every party manager,—if, what I know not, a wire-puller ever gives a moment to meditation. There is, indeed, a risk that the changes, the shiftings, the conversions and re-conversions, of public men may lead the English people to hold statesmen, of whatever party, as cheap as Americans hold "politicians." This danger affects all parties alike; but what candid man can say that, in point of character, Conservatives compare unfavourably with the members of the Gladstonian Opposition? Each party has its black sheep; of these let us say little.

For the rest, Englishmen trust Mr. Balfour just as much as they once trusted Sir George Trevelyan; Mr. W. H. Smith inspires at least as much confidence as Mr. John Morley; there is no reason why Mr. Goschen—to put the matter very mildly—should be deemed a less competent Chancellor of the Exchequer than Sir William Harcourt. Character, wherever it be wanting, is the admitted possession of the Liberal Unionists. The deep discredit which the Maamtrasna debate, and all the memories it evokes, has inflicted in different ways and in different degrees on every other Parliamentary connection, does not touch Lord Hartington and his followers. They can give weight enough to any party which receives their countenance. It is, however, far from my purpose to dwell much in these letters on the personal aspects of politics. What I do insist upon is that the situation, the principles, and the character of existing political divisions make it idle to apply to them a maxim which had a real application to the conflicts between the Whigs and Tories of a past generation. Rhetoric, sanctified by tradition, now lacks all the ring of reality, and the orators who honestly employ it mistake dreams suggested by historical reminiscence for the realities of actual life.

The doctrine, again, that the alliance of Liberals with Conservatives is in itself disgraceful, is nothing less than the maxim of the duty of passive obedience to the dictation of partisanship.

The preachers of this dogma, however carefully they veil their meaning, betray their own fundamental misconception of the nature and cogency of party obligations. In a country such as England, honest party differences rest on the tacit recognition by all Englishmen of the fact that we are all bound together by deep and essential agreement on the main principles of government. In lands where such fundamental concord has no existence, party government, as we know it, is an impossibility. One cause why the revolutions of France have no end, is that rival factions are really enemies battling over the foundations of the Constitution. Republicans proscribe Conservatives because a French Conservative is a reactionary whose mission it is not to preserve, but to destroy the Republic. Conservatives cannot tolerate moderate Republicanism, because they know that a Republican Ministry must aim at the destruction of Conservative influences, and because they do not concede to the Republic the moral right to allegiance; they remember that Republicans used the victories of foreigners to destroy a national Government, and that the Commune burst into insurrection when Prussian armies were camped round Paris. With us it is far otherwise. Party combinations are recognised as instruments—awkward instruments at the best—for carrying into effect the will of the nation. Party loyalty, while rightly honoured as a check on the pursuit of private interest, or on the indulgence of individual caprice, is, in the judgment of fair-minded citizens, limited by at least two conditions. Allegiance to party must not, in the first place, interfere with allegiance to the nation; hence in periods of invasion, of insurrection, and, but for recent experience, I should have added of wide resistance to the authority of law, men of every political creed are expected to rally round the Executive,— come what will, "the Queen's Government," as people used to say, "must be carried on." Zeal for party, in the second place, is no plea for a partisan's toleration of what he deems public immorality. Hence the deep respect felt by men who, like myself, cannot share John Bright's views on foreign policy, for his honest protest against what he deemed the sin of the Crimean War; hence the infinite gratitude felt by hundreds of Liberals for his equally honest protest against sympathy with slave-owners, defended though that sympathy was by the plea that oligarchical rebellion against a Republic had created an independent nation. Each of these limitations is fatal to the doctrine of unrestricted party loyalty. Each of these limitations fully justifies Liberal Unionists in the support of a Unionist and Conservative Government. The nation is threatened with peril as grave as open insurrection, and far more insidious; the maintenance of national unity is the highest and most pressing of duties. Precedents are needless, yet two precedents are well worth notice. My friend Mr. E. L. Godkin, of New York, is a keen and most impressive assailant of Unionist policy; but to friends who know his career, the example of his acts is more instructive than the acuteness of his criticism. His noble efforts created the Independents of the United States, diverted them from the Republican Party, and induced them, for the sake of a great national object, to elect a Democratic President. He did well, and Liberal Unionists —the Independents of England—will do equally well to imitate his conduct. From Gladstonians, again, we have heard much of Burke; little reference have they made to the most important transaction of Burke's life. The "bottomless Whig" broke the Whig Party to fragments, because in his judgment the eloquence, the recklessness, the imprudence, and the sanguine enthusiasm of Fox, were leading the country into the paths of political immorality and national ruin. The Old Whig saw nothing blameworthy in support of a Tory Ministry.

To denounce all co-operation between Liberals and Conservatives is, lastly, to contradict the fundamental axiom of popular government.

This matter deserves a moment's attention. Democracy rests on the sovereignty of the people,—or, in other words, on the acknowledged supremacy of the permanent will of the nation as expressed by the voice of the majority. With this principle, party government, as understood in England, has always a tendency to conflict; but the collision between the wishes of a faction and the wish of the people is avoided or mitigated by the looseness of party discipline. On many points a minority among Liberals will often, with more or less activity, support Conservative policy, or a minority among Conservatives support a Liberal policy. Hence, by a rough and awkward process, the will of the nation is enforced against the will of a minority who claim power as the majority amongst the members of the most powerful of two political parties. Palmerston was no Radical. Towards the close of his career, the majority of earnest Liberals would not have kept him in power. He retained office in virtue of the tacit sympathy existing between many Liberals and many Conservatives. There were Tories who preferred him to Disraeli; there were Liberals who dreaded the leadership of

Gladstone or of Bright. The nation obtained the Minister who was desired by the nation. If the rules of party loyalty be made so rigid that co-operation by the members of one political party with the members of another becomes an impossibility, then the result inevitably follows that a body of men may rule who admittedly do not represent the views held by the majority of the nation. At this very moment, the citizens of the United Kingdom have pronounced against Home Rule. Yet, if the Liberal Unionists adopt the notion that co-operation with Conservatives is disgraceful, a measure of Home Rule will of a certainty be carried. The majority of the Liberal Party will triumph over the nation. This may be right or may be wrong, but this is not popular government; and such triumph of the minority on a question of vital importance would make democrats demand innovations which would place the main institutions of the country and the leading principles of the Constitution on a foundation where they could not be shaken by the devices of party managers. However this may be, to stretch tightly the bonds of party allegiance is assuredly to risk a conflict between the desire of a faction and the will of the nation.

The maxim, then, of "no alliance with Tories" need not trouble Unionists. It derives currency from a misinterpretation of existing political opinion; it is based on a false notion of party loyalty; it conflicts with the sovereignty of the nation.

LETTER VII

ON THE TWO ALLIANCES

CHARACTER is power; loss of reputation is loss of authority.

This is a truth attested by every page from the annals of England. It well deserves the consideration of Liberal Unionists. They are tormented by scruples about co-operation with Conservatives; they are depressed by disappointment at isolated defeats; they are tried by impatience at temporary reverses; they are perplexed at finding that the party which defends the rights of the people need not for the moment be the party of popularity. Alliance of one kind or another is, they rightly feel, a necessity ;. in politics, permanent isolation is final ruin. Two combinations are offered to their choice. The option presented is co-operation with Conservatives, or coalition with Parnellites; no other choice is open. From the first some honest Unionists are repelled, because it is called a surrender to Toryism; towards the second they are attracted, because it is styled the restoration of Liberal unity. Let me try for a moment to get behind phrases, and test the meaning of words by the very truth of facts. Let me insist upon the maxim that, with Englishmen, "character is power," and, guided by my firm belief in its absolute truth, show why it counsels friendship with Conservatives as the path of safety, and warns every true Unionist from the Gladstonian or Parnellite alliance as from sure destruction.

Co-operation between Liberal Unionists and Conservative Unionists brings no discredit upon either Liberals or Tories. Of principle there is no compromise whatever. As to the end to be pursued, there is absolute agreement; to every Unionist, the maintenance of national unity is of supreme importance. Nor does any vital difference exist as to the right means for the attainment of a common end; no Unionist disputes that every citizen of the United Kingdom must enjoy the free exercise of his legal rights, and that, therefore, the law must be enforced throughout the length and breadth of the land; no one in the Unionist ranks questions that the Courts ought to obtain the same obedience in Cork or in Kerry as in Midlothian or in Middlesex; no Unionist of weight doubts that the grievances of Irish tenants, so far as they can be remedied by law, ought to be redressed, or that the tenure of land is the source of Irish discontent; nor does it lie upon Unionists to dispute that Mr. Gladstone's land legislation has failed, partly from its inherent faults, partly from the neglect to enforce that obedience to law which is a necessary condition for any successful reform in the tenure of land

In the desire to abolish dual ownership, Unionists are at one; they are also at one in the belief that a policy of reform must be a policy of honesty, and that landlords have the same rights as other British subjects. In this matter it is not the bigotry of Conservatism which need excite disquiet. The danger is not that too much, but that too little respect may be paid to rights conferred by law. There is, again, no ground for alleging essential disagreement between Unionists as to matters lying beyond the limits of Irish policy. It is, of course, idle to fancy a kind of unanimity which does not exist; it were folly to imagine that Lord Salisbury is in all or in most questions of the same mind with Mr. Chamberlain; and no man of honour or of sense would wish for a sham agreement; from Tory Democrats or from democratic Tories little benefit can be expected by the English nation. But in matters of statesmanship, speculative agreement is not needed. All that is necessary is that political allies should honestly agree on the mode of dealing with subjects which imperatively require to be handled; some questions must wait for their solution till the battle for national unity is fought out and won; no sane statesman bent on defending the Union would now raise a controversy as to Disestablishment. A Ministry which is truly national will seek to meet the demands of the nation. Many questions exist which can be settled in accordance with something like national agreement. The Land Laws may be reformed, the sphere of local self-government may be extended, the complaints of agricultural labourers may be met, Colonial goodwill may be fostered, a policy of quiet progress at home and of peaceful independence abroad may be maintained, by a Ministry who rely on the support of a party resolved to forego the attainment of objects specially desired by Tories or by Liberals, in order to repel an assault on the political integrity of the nation. No doubt the leaders of such a party must abstain from great organic changes in the Constitution. But the mass of the people, now that democracy is triumphant, care far more for social improvements than for constitutional innovation. No calm observer can fail to see that a party containing at once a Conservative and a Liberal element, approaches social problems at a great advantage. In what manner Liberal Unionists may best aid a Unionist Ministry, is a question to be left to the decision of honoured and trusted leaders. Implicit reliance may be placed on the manly honesty of Lord Hartington and the moral intuitions of Mr. Bright. Co-operation between men who have hitherto belonged to different parties has indeed its obvious inconveniences. But it has its compensating benefits. An alliance based on concern for national interest, if it breaks down the lines of party connection, revives a sense of allegiance to the nation; it is an alliance which, if it requires some sacrifice of private feelings, involves no loss of character; it adds to the repute and may double the strength of English statesmanship.

Alliance with Gladstonians and Parnellites is nothing else than surrender by Unionists of all attempt to defend the Union. Respect for a distinguished career forbids the supposition that Mr. Gladstone would consent to lead the Liberal Party on condition of renouncing the policy of Home Rule. Such a renunciation would either betray a laxity of principle of which he is incapable, or involve the confession of such an error of judgment as would disqualify him for leadership. Assume, however, that Unionists were willing to surrender the Union, or could accept a compromise, are they willing to pay the price of the Parnellite alliance? What this price is we know by experience. The career of the Gladstonians tells the result of a coalition between a body of constitutional Liberals and a body of revolutionary Separatists. The Gladstonians came to terms with the Parnellites under favourable conditions; Mr. Gladstone was an honest convert to Home Rule; his followers brought themselves to believe that they believed in the creed of their leader; Mr. Gladstone's immense influence held out the hope that the Parnellites might become Gladstonians, and that under constitutional guidance revolutionists might adopt constitutional methods. What has happened is matter of history. English Liberals have from the necessity of things followed the lead of their Irish confederates. Gladstonians, headed by a trained Parliamentarian, once reverenced Parliamentary government; they have now sanctioned tactics which destroy the dignity and menace the authority of Parliament. Not long ago they rated high the rights of property and the claims of individual freedom, and, with Burke, entertained "no idea of liberty unconnected with honesty and justice;" they have now given to the "Plan of Campaign," resting as it does on theft and oppression, first the consent of ominous silence, next the countenance of mild reprehension, then the benefit of sophistic apology, and lastly, the stimulus of all but applausive sympathy. Time was when Liberalism plumed itself on cultivated intelligence and high independence; of recent days, Liberal doctrine has inculcated on the uneducated masses that ignorance may neglect the guidance of knowledge, and Liberal sympathy, by soothing the conscience of Irish agitators, has involved English politicians in the worst guilt of Parnellism. For in the day of national judgment, the heaviest charge brought by history against the Parnellites will not be that they have injured England—for England they have regarded, and from their own point of view, not without justification, as a foe—but that they have inflicted deadly wrong upon Ireland. Their unpardonable offence is the moral degradation of the people whom they meant to serve. In this they stand in hideous contrast with the patriots of past days. Grattan and the Volunteers, O'Connell and the Repealers, Smith O'Brien and Young Ireland, all strove to found national independence upon the elevation of national morality. For the heroes of the Land League it was reserved to recommend to an impoverished peasantry covetousness, cruelty, and suspicion, as sentiments to be nurtured by patriots desirous of new national life. To sit by while landlords are attacked, as though to be a landlord was to be a criminal, to allow or suffer the denunciation of hirers or purchasers of land as "land-grabbers," is, say what apologists will, to countenance immorality. Teach a tenant that it is laudable to covet his neighbour's land, if that neighbour be a landlord; teach him that it is a duty to steal, if only the money stolen be rent,—and it is not in human nature but that he should improve upon the lesson. He has learnt that it is a duty to violate the eighth and tenth commandments; he will infer that it is no heavy sin to break the sixth or the ninth. Respect for law and hatred of violence have hitherto been the proud characteristic of English Liberalism; under the influence of the Parnellite alliance, Liberals have assaulted the character of the Bench, have questioned the impartiality of juries, have palliated outrage, have shrunk from every effort to strengthen the action of the law, and have used language which suggests that the tribunals of the League possess a higher moral authority than the Courts of the Queen. Gladstonians have in truth at times gone further, and have avowed the favourite dogma of revolution,—that law is of no obligation on any man who challenges its justice. What, again, has become of the seriousness which once marked English statesmanship? Plain men are astounded at the levity or light-heartedness of reputable politicians; deliberate assertions of responsible officials are lightly held of no account; grave charges, made by respected Judges, are lightly set aside as entitled to small respect; to underrate the capacity of the magistracy, or to charge the law itself with injustice, is deemed a trifle. Meanwhile, the vehement contradictions of unscrupulous partisanship are esteemed worthy of credit, and elaborate arguments are based on the offhand denial of notorious facts; statesmen of high character believe with easy credulity, and assert with confident readiness, that men who but a year or two ago needed to be checked in the career of crime by all the resources of civilisation, have now undergone a permanent change in their words, actions, and convictions. Whoever, after glancing at a few numbers of *United Ireland*, or after reading the recent speeches delivered at the Rotunda, can believe "that Irishmen" and (Irishmen must be taken here to mean Parnellites) "look to political means for reform and the redress of grievances, and that their object is no longer to defy, but to persuade and conciliate their countrymen on this side the Channel," may well enough place faith in the sudden and permanent transformation of revolutionary conspiracy into lawful agitation. But to an observer under no temptation to take the strength of a wish as the guarantee for its own fulfilment, "conversions" which would be suspicious in the realm of religion are incredible in the world of politics. Nor to such an one will the assertion that Ireland is filled with strong, vivid, and buoyant hope bear conviction; one thing it does prove,—namely, that Gladstonians see the darkest objects in the light thrown upon them by the reviving hope of Gladstonian triumph. This sanguine disposition is favoured by boundless capacity for the substitution of words for facts;

boycotting is stripped of all its odiousness by being dubbed with the comparatively respectable *alias* of "exclusive dealing"; on a similar principle, assassinations which have made the Phœnix Park a place of horror may some day be freed from obloquy by being called "acts of warfare." To men who sincerely wish to palliate actions which their conscience condemns, such changes of name may give true comfort; but Englishmen or Irishmen who note the condition of public opinion, will feel deep alarm at the facility with which statesmen of ability and virtue play with language in order that they may ignore facts. Nor are the pleas which candour urges in defence of the conduct of Gladstonian Liberalism reassuring. "Respectable Liberals disapproved obstruction." So be it; but the disapproval was silent, and the party profited by the indiscretions of its more violent members; that the receiver is worse than the thief, is a maxim of wide application, and extends to matters not within the jurisdiction of the Old Bailey. "Approval of Irish agitation is expressed with many reserves, and subject to many conditions." Provisos and reservations may save the character of the speaker, but in no way tell on the effect of the speech; every boycotter in Ireland can say and believe with plausibility, if not with truth, that his system of exclusive dealing has the sanction of Mr. Gladstone, and every boycotter in Ireland will take comfort. "Mr. Gladstone and many of his followers are influenced by good motives, and are men of high character." I admit that this is so. The admission is part of my argument; my very case is that excellent persons who coalesce with revolutionists catch in spite of themselves the revolutionary disease, and are compelled to adopt revolutionary methods. What has befallen one branch of the Liberal Party would, under like circumstances, befall the other. Let Liberal Unionists who dread the contact of Toryism, look on the Gladstonians and see the result of alliance with Parnellites. The Gladstonians boast they are gaining in numbers. So be it; they are nevertheless losing the reputation which is the ultimate source of authority.

The matter, then, stands thus:—Liberal Unionists may co-operate with Conservatives, and thus, at the price of possibly retarding specific Liberal reforms, preserve the unity of the nation and maintain the traditions of Liberalism. They may, by alliance with Parnellites, hasten some Liberal reforms at the price of breaking up the national unity, and sacrificing that weight of character which is the true foundation of power and authority.

LETTER VIII

CONCLUSION

My analysis of Unionist delusions is at an end; let me sum up its results and point its lesson.

It is a delusion that the "concessions" hoped for or extorted from Mr. Gladstone can reunite the Liberal Party. Of these concessions, the one threatens dishonour to the English nation, the other entails weakness on the English Parliament. The sole concession which might put an end to the dissent of Liberal Unionists, is Mr. Gladstone's honest conversion from the Home-Rule heresy. Such a change of faith is a moral impossibility; it would of itself disqualify Mr. Gladstone for the position of a party leader.[1]

It is a delusion to suppose that the Home-Rule controversy can be terminated with satisfaction to Unionists by a compromise or transaction. A true compromise is an impossibility. Maintenance of the Union and the Parliamentary independence of Ireland are opposed to each other no less in fact than in logic. A sham compromise is merely a misguiding name for the concession to Ireland of a narrow, restricted form of Home Rule. But in this matter half-measures are rash measures; if Ireland is to obtain Home Rule, it is the interest no less of Great Britain than of Ireland that she should receive the widest measure of Parliamentary independence compatible with the safety of Great Britain; on this point—though on this point alone—my opinion appears to be supported by the authority of Sir Charles Gavan Duffy. A compromise is in principle

[1] See Letter I.

a surrender, and a surrender, which for the sake of appearing to be a compromise, is made on terms which deprive concession at once of its grace and of its possible benefits.[1]

It is a delusion to draw from the undoubted fact that Separation is opposed to the true interests of Ireland,—first, the hazardous inference that Irishmen will never desire national independence, and next, the demonstrably groundless conclusion that Home Rule in Ireland threatens no serious danger to England. At each point the argument breaks down. Irishmen, like other human beings, often entertain wishes opposed to their true interest; hence Irishmen may well desire Separation. The very circumstances, moreover, which forbid Ireland to claim national independence must suggest, and, indeed, have suggested, to Irishmen the expediency of dissolving the United Kingdom into a Confederation; but Federalism is far more dangerous to England

[1] See Letter II.

than Irish independence. Home Rule, then, either means Separation, or else means national disintegration. Separation is the loss of a limb; Federalism means assured paralysis and probable death.[1]

It is a delusion to dream that Home Rule in Ireland will bring peace to England; it will ensure disquiet, it threatens protracted revolution.[2]

It is a delusion to hold that the movement in favour of Home Rule may be, so to speak, outflanked by extending to Ireland a system of extended Local Self-Government. Extended municipal franchises are a totally different thing from Home Rule. Hence the widest scheme of Local Self-Government will never meet the desires of Nationalists. That it will confer any benefit on Ireland is open to the gravest doubt; that it must weaken the hands of the Executive Government, and thus increase the difficulties of England, is a certainty.[3]

---

[1] See Letter III. [2] See Letter IV. [3] See Letter V.

It is a delusion to imagine that the co-operation of Liberals with Conservatives in defence of national unity is a disgrace. Whoever adopts the watchword, "No alliance with Tories," misunderstands the nature and objects of modern party divisions, places the interest of a faction above the welfare of the State, and contradicts the fundamental axiom of popular government,—the doctrine of the sovereignty of the people. Politicians, moreover, who shudder at co-operation between Liberals and Tories, forget that Unionists must in the long run accept the friendship of Lord Salisbury or alliance with Mr. Parnell. Co-operation with Lord Salisbury entails, it may be, inconvenience, but involves no loss of character; coalition with Mr. Parnell will bring on Liberal Unionists, as it has brought on Gladstonians, all the deserved disrepute which falls upon constitutionalists when they adopt the ends and sanction the methods of revolutionists and law-breakers. Character in England is strength; the party which in moments of trial and at all costs preserves character, ensures for itself in the future the certainty of influence and of power.[1]

To escape from delusions is to recognise truth, and Unionists who escape from the dominion of fallacies generated in the main by half-heartedness, will soon, amidst all the perplexities and entanglements of the present situation, discern where lies for them the path of honour and of wisdom, and what are the virtues which must specially be cultivated by men bent upon travelling along an arduous road towards a noble goal. Concessions, compromises, or transactions are ruin; a bold adoption of the boldest form of Home Rule, or the resolute defence of national unity, are the only alternatives worthy of consideration by any man of sense and vigour. No honest Unionist can, unless under the necessity imposed by crushing and final defeat, advocate Home Rule. Every

---

[1] See Letters VI. and VII.

honest Unionist will therefore now, during the time of battle and (despite small failures) of success, decline to hear of parleyings, conferences, or negotiations. Every Unionist must stand firm by the Union. But the defence of national unity, while it is the first, will not appear to any Unionist to be the sole duty of the day. To the complaints or aspirations of the labouring classes throughout every part of the United Kingdom, it behoves statesmen to give a willing and intelligent hearing. Wise men of all parties now accept the fact that to settle finally on fair terms the tenure of land in Ireland is to go to the root of Irish difficulties. To achieve such a settlement is the highest duty and the highest interest of Unionists; their leaders are the only body of statesmen who can hope to perform this gigantic task; they entertain no idea either of liberty or of generosity which is unconnected with honesty and justice; they therefore can carry through a measure of reform without letting it degenerate into a scheme of violence and confiscation, they will sternly enforce law because law is justice, and will take care that innovations carried out for the sake of national objects shall be made at the cost of the nation. Unionists, again, will know that the virtues which the times imperatively demand are firmness, constancy, and moderation. To the small but honoured body of men on whose steadfastness depends the welfare of the nation, each Unionist will give his unqualified support. He will not let himself be elated by trifles; he will not fancy the country lost because Mr. Brunner can add his vote to the forces of obstruction; he will not think the battle for the Union finished because Mr. Fellowes can now shout, "Hear, hear!" when Mr. Robertson exposes the fallacies of the Opposition. To Unionists, indeed, worthy of the cause in which they are enrolled, even mischances will not always appear unmixed evils. The energy — the laudable energy — of Irish Members has turned and will turn English elections. These triumphs of Parnellism are in themselves deplorable; but the particular development of Irish activity should be hailed with infinite satisfaction. Every time a Parnellite addresses an English constituency, he undermines his own cause; he imitates Hogarth's elector who, drunk with zeal for his candidate, cuts through the signboard on which he himself is seated. His conduct confutes his principles. In the House of Commons he may shout, "I am an alien," but by his appearance on the hustings he exercises his rights as a member of the United Kingdom, and proclaims that he is a citizen of the greatest and freest among European States. There is not, again, any reason to lament that a score of young Conservatives or Liberals should leave the sittings of Parliament that they may meet their Irish opponents face to face before the electors of England. The fuss and fury of a canvass are an evil; but that English politicians should accustom themselves to express in plain language the plain thoughts which tell with a popular audience, is a good, and a great good. From an honest interchange of ideas between honest English gentlemen and honest English voters, nothing but good can ensue. If the country labourers or town artisans gain much, the speakers who address rustics and workmen gain more. It is far better that youthful Unionists should learn from Mr. T. P. O'Connor in contests on the hustings the secret of popular eloquence and popular argument, than that in the House of Commons they should learn pompous jocosity from Sir William Harcourt, or brutal manners from Dr. Tanner. English imitation of Irish energy might well be carried further. The first body of English Members who plead the Unionist cause at an Irish election will render a memorable service to the country. Their labours will not immediately win votes, but their boldness and toil will not be thrown away, for the presence of English politicians at an Irish election will prove to electors— who, whatever their faults, are not dull-witted — that to Englishmen the whole United Kingdom is a common country. To look at the brighter side of a dark prospect is, it must be admitted, if a necessary, not always an easy achievement. Opponents who detest Mr. Gladstone's policy may admire his unbounded hopefulness; it is full of instruction. When General Grant first commanded an army, he was, he tells us, depressed by the constant effort to anticipate the possible moves of a skilful opponent. His anxiety found relief when he at last became impressed with the conviction that the Confederate commander was probably at that moment tormented by the attempt to anticipate the movements of General Grant. He thereupon gave his mind in calmness to making the most of his own advantages. In any great contest, advantages of position and of fortune are more or less equally distributed. For Unionists, the great thing is to realise their own strength. On the side of the Separatists are all the arts of rhetoric, and all the gains conferred by specious phrases; they have at their head a leader of admitted talent and of undoubted enthusiasm, who can always cover poverty of thought with exuberance of words, and weakness of argument with copiousness of sophism, and of sophism the more dangerous because it has imposed on the speaker's own judgment. Separatists have appealed, and with success, to some of the meanest and to some of the best parts of human nature. They have appealed to ignorance, to levity, to hopefulness, to sympathy, and to generosity. Who shall deny the power of these sentiments ? Unionists count, indeed, on their side, the greatest living master of English speech; but though he shows the fire, he no longer possesses the physical energy of youth. They must, therefore, meet rhetoric not by eloquence, but by plain statement of truth. Nor is the cause they advocate one which directly arouses popular emotion. Still, they have on their side most powerful allies. Knowledge is stronger than ignorance. Sense and reason are meant to control, and—incredible though it may appear—do in the long run control the impetuousness of sentiment. Indignation at wrongdoing and resentment at oppression, even though the oppression be exercised by the poor, and be miscalled "exclusive dealing," are as legitimate and as powerful emotions as sympathy with suffering or pity for distress. Generosity is one of the graces of human life; but common honesty and common justice ought to curb, and can curb, the impulses of generosity, for common honesty and common justice are strong with all the strength which governs the universe.

THE END

MESSRS. MACMILLAN AND CO.'S PUBLICATIONS.

BY THE SAME AUTHOR.

Lectures Introductory to the Study of the Law of the Constitution. Second Edition. Demy 8vo. 12s. 6d.

Mr. GLADSTONE said in his speech in the House of Commons on 8th April 1886:—"I do not know whether many gentlemen here may have read the valuable work of Professor Dicey on 'The Law of the Constitution.' No work I ever read brings out in a more distinct and emphatic manner the peculiarity of the British Constitution in one point, to which, perhaps, we seldom have occasion to refer, viz. the absolute supremacy of Parliament."

The MARQUIS OF HARTINGTON said in the House of Commons on 9th April 1886:—"I conceive that the constitutional condition of the Queen is a portion of the Imperial Legislature, and the definition which I have given of the sovereign power in this country is one derived from the work which was referred to yesterday by my right hon. friend, that of Professor Dicey on the Constitution, and to that book I will refer the hon. member [Mr. Healy], if he thinks there is anything disloyal in the language I have just spoken."

The Privy Council. Crown 8vo. 3s. 6d.

The Irish Union. A History of the Legislative Union of Great Britain and Ireland. By T. Dunbar Ingram, LL.D., of Lincoln's Inn, Barrister-at-Law, formerly Professor of Jurisprudence, and of Hindu and Muhammedan Law in the Presidency College, Calcutta. Demy 8vo. 10s. 6d.

Mr. JOHN BRIGHT, in a letter to the *Times*, 8th August, 1887, says:—"I have read Mr. Dunbar Ingram's book with great interest, and hope it may be widely read. . . . Mr. Ingram's excellent book will be very useful with all who can read and reason upon the great contest which is now before us."

By J. R. SEELEY, M.A., Regius Professor of Modern History in the University of Cambridge.

Lectures and Essays. 8vo. 10s. 6d.

The Expansion of England. Two Courses of Lectures. Crown 8vo. 4s. 6d.

The *Times* says:—"These lectures deserve the closest and most intelligent attention. Their appearance at a time when vital questions of foreign and colonial policy are pressing for a solution is most opportune. . . . The little volume is well worth careful study, were it only in the view of suggesting intelligent objections, and so ventilating questions of the most vital importance."

Our Colonial Expansion. Extracts from the *Expansion of England*. Crown 8vo. 1s.

Letters from Donegal in 1886. By a Lady "Felon." Edited by Colonel Maurice, Professor of Military History, Royal Staff College. Crown 8vo. Price 6d.

The *Spectator* says:—"They give us the best, because wholly unpremeditated, evidence as to how loyal Ulster views the present crisis."

The *Times* says:—"A little book which at the present crisis is likely to be very acceptable to the reading and thinking public. . . . The letters treat in an exceptionally interesting manner the present relations between Irish peasant and Landlord, and between Catholic and Protestant."

MACMILLAN AND CO., LONDON.

MESSRS. MACMILLAN AND CO.'S PUBLICATIONS.

By JOHN RICHARD GREEN, M.A., LL.D.

A Short History of the English People. With Coloured Maps, Genealogical Tables, and Chronological Annals. Crown 8vo. 8s. 6d. 126th Thousand.

History of the English People. In four vols. 8vo. Vol. I. EARLY ENGLAND, 449-1071—Foreign Kings, 1071-1214—The Charter, 1204-1291—The Parliament, 1307-1461. With Eight Coloured Maps. 8vo. 16s.—Vol. II. The Monarchy, 1461-1540—The Reformation, 1540-1603. 8vo. 16s.—Vol. III. Puritan England, 1603-1660—The Revolution, 1660-1688. With Four Maps. 8vo. 16s.—Vol. IV. The Revolution, 1683-1760.—Modern England, 1760-1815. With Maps and Index. 8vo. 16s.

The Making of England. With Maps. 8vo. 16s.

The Conquest of England. With Maps and Portraits. 8vo. 18s.

TWENTY-FOURTH YEAR OF PUBLICATION
(Revised after Official Returns) of the
STATESMAN'S YEAR-BOOK;

A Statistical and Historical Annual of the States of the Civilised World for the Year 1887. Edited by J. SCOTT KELTIE, Librarian to the Royal Geographical Society. Crown 8vo. 10s. 6d.

"As indispensable as Bradshaw."—*Times.*

The *Times* says:—"The work steadily maintains its high character as a book of reference for all who are interested by occupation or disposition in public affairs."

Now Ready, in Crown 8vo, Price 3s. 6d. each.

"An important series of volumes on practical politics and legislation."—*Daily News.*

"An admirable idea."—*British Quarterly Review.*

"In this series the public have the means of acquiring a great deal of information, which it would be difficult to find in so convenient a form elsewhere."—*St. James's Gazette.*

𝔗𝔥𝔢 𝔈𝔫𝔤𝔩𝔦𝔰𝔥 ℭ𝔦𝔱𝔦𝔷𝔢𝔫:

A Series of short books on his rights and responsibilities.
Edited by HENRY CRAIK, C.B., M.A. Oxon., LL.D. Glasgow.

The following are the Titles of the Volumes:—

Central Government. H. D. TRAILL, D.C.L.

The Electorate and the Legislature. SPENCER WALPOLE.

Local Government. M. D. CHALMERS.

The National Budget: The National Debt, Taxes, and Rates. A. J. WILSON.

The State in its Relation to Education. HENRY CRAIK, C.B., M.A., LL.D

The Poor Law. Rev. T. W. FOWLE, M.A.

The State in Relation to Labour. W. STANLEY JEVONS, LL.D., M.A., F.R.S.

The State in Relation to Trade. Sir T. H. FARRER, Bart.

The State and the Church. Hon. A. D. ELLIOT, M.P.

The Land Laws. Professor F. POLLOCK.

Foreign Relations. SPENCER WALPOLE.

Colonies and Dependencies. Part I. INDIA. By J. S. COTTON, M.A. Part II. THE COLONIES. By E. J. PAYNE, M.A.

Justice and Police. By F. W. MAITLAND.

The Punishment and Prevention of Crime. By Colonel Sir EDMUND F. DU CANE, K.C.B., R.E.

MACMILLAN AND CO., LONDON.

www.ingramcontent.com/pod-product-compliance
Lightning Source LLC
Chambersburg PA
CBHW031353160426
43196CB00007B/802